Fail
Safe

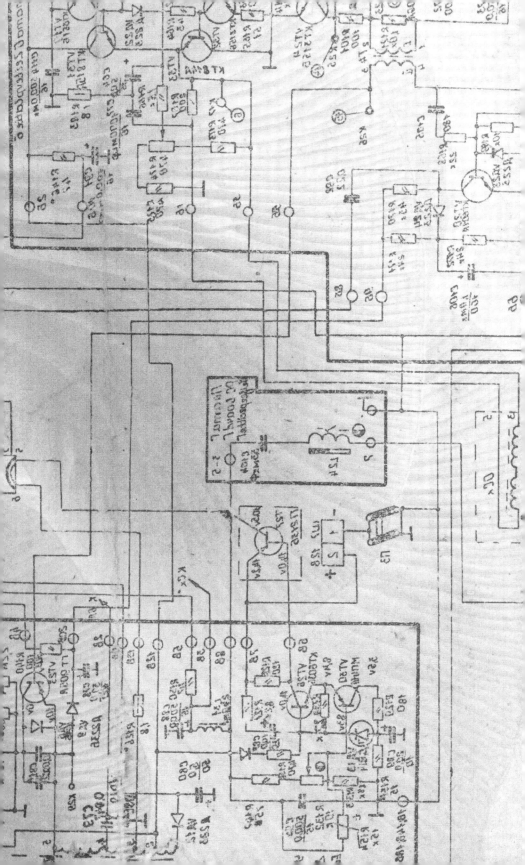

UNIVERSITY OF CALGARY
Press

Fail Safe

NIKKI SHEPPY

Brave & Brilliant Series
ISSN 2371-7238 (Print) ISSN 2371-7246 (Online)

University of Calgary Press
2500 University Drive NW
Calgary, Alberta
Canada T2N 1N4

press.ucalgary.ca

LIBRARY AND ARCHIVES CANADA CATALOGUING IN PUBLICATION

Sheppy, Nikki, author
    Fail safe / Nikki Sheppy.

(Brave & brilliant series, 2371-7238 ; 3)
Poems.
Issued in print and electronic formats.
ISBN 978-1-55238-963-8 (softcover).—ISBN 978-1-55238-964-5
(PDF).—ISBN 978-1-55238-965-2 (EPUB).—ISBN 978-1-55238-966-9
(Kindle)

    I. Title. II. Series: Brave & brilliant series ; 3

PS8637.H47875F35 2017   C811'.6   C2017-906678-1
                                            C2017-906679-X

The University of Calgary Press acknowledges the support of the Government of Alberta
through the Alberta Media Fund for our publications. We acknowledge the financial
support of the Government of Canada. We acknowledge the financial support of the
Canada Council for the Arts for our publishing program.

Printed and bound in Canada by Marquis
♻ This book is printed on Rolland Opaque Smooth Natural FSC paper

Cover images: #1278885 and #7118608 (colourbox.com)
Editing by Helen Hajnoczky
Cover design, page design, and typesetting by Melina Cusano

I wanted to write a book that did not derive its structural unity from free verse, but from a horde of words: a protective mechanism borne deep inside it, but with maximum freedom, and mobility

—*Chus Pato, tr. Erín Moure*

HOW TO READ

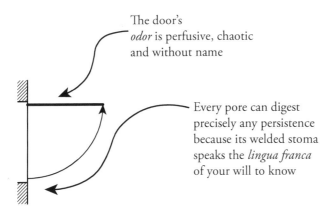

The door's
odor is perfusive, chaotic
and without name

Every pore can digest
precisely any persistence
because its welded stoma
speaks the *lingua franca*
of your will to know

adore = thresh hold
berating, infolding

The way I have entered & been entered, this is
architecture. The way I have dwelled & plotted egress,
this is architecture. The sweep of my leaving, star-
saving breast tracing a quarter circuit
of my revolution, this is architecture.

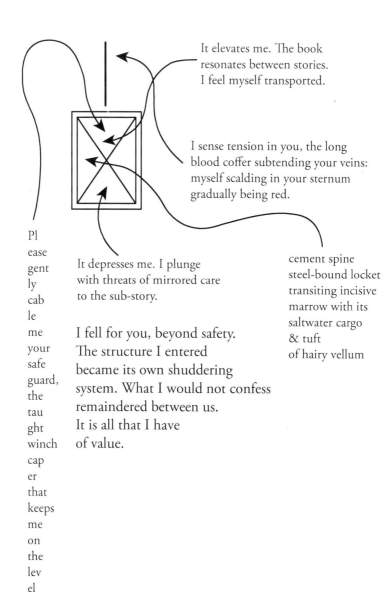

It elevates me. The book resonates between stories. I feel myself transported.

I sense tension in you, the long blood coffer subtending your veins: myself scalding in your sternum gradually being red.

Pl
ease
gent
ly
cab
le
me
your
safe
guard,
the
tau
ght
winch
cap
er
that
keeps
me
on
the
lev
el

It depresses me. I plunge with threats of mirrored care to the sub-story.

I fell for you, beyond safety. The structure I entered became its own shuddering system. What I would not confess remaindered between us. It is all that I have of value.

cement spine
steel-bound locket
transiting incisive
marrow with its
saltwater cargo
& tuft
of hairy vellum

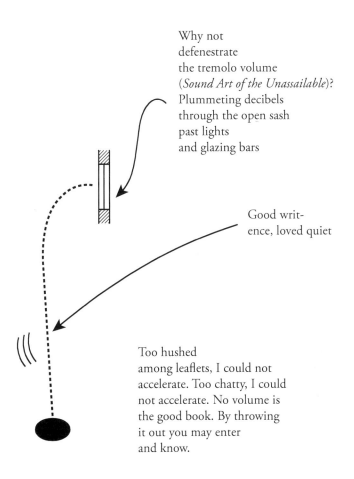

Why not
defenestrate
the tremolo volume
(*Sound Art of the Unassailable*)?
Plummeting decibels
through the open sash
past lights
and glazing bars

Good writ-
ence, loved quiet

Too hushed
among leaflets, I could not
accelerate. Too chatty, I could
not accelerate. No volume is
the good book. By throwing
it out you may enter
and know.

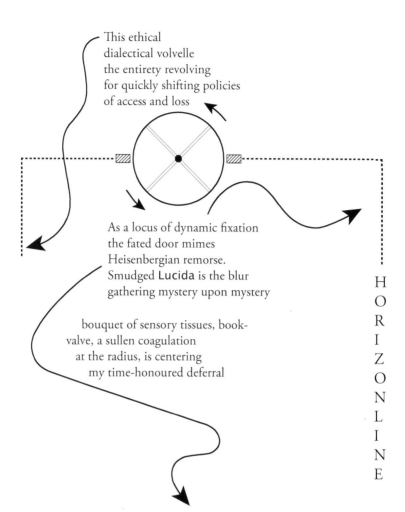

This ethical
dialectical volvelle
the entirety revolving
for quickly shifting policies
of access and loss

As a locus of dynamic fixation
the fated door mimes
Heisenbergian remorse.
Smudged **Lucida** is the blur
gathering mystery upon mystery

bouquet of sensory tissues, book-
valve, a sullen coagulation
at the radius, is centering
my time-honoured deferral

H
O
R
I
Z
O
N
L
I
N
E

Reaching for the silken levers
radiating from my own shoulders
I flowed between risk
and harrowing shelter

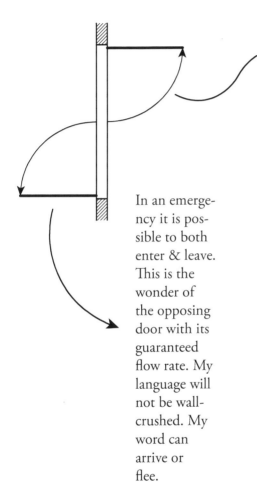

Either way,
with throbbed
looking askance,
an ampersand, an
unlikely allen key
edged with facets
that pour into
my syllables

In an emerge-
ncy it is pos-
sible to both
enter & leave.
This is the
wonder of
the opposing
door with its
guaranteed
flow rate. My
language will
not be wall-
crushed. My
word can
arrive or
flee.

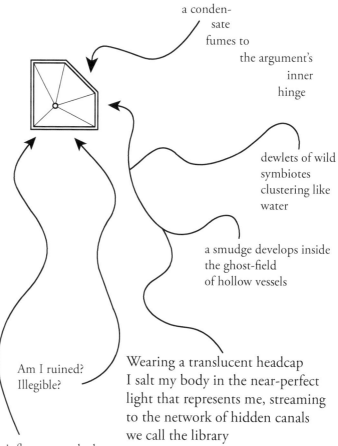

a conden-
sate
fumes to
the argument's
inner
hinge

dewlets of wild
symbiotes
clustering like
water

a smudge develops inside
the ghost-field
of hollow vessels

Am I ruined?
Illegible?

Wearing a translucent headcap
I salt my body in the near-perfect
light that represents me, streaming
to the network of hidden canals
we call the library

The inflorescence sheds
itself. Traces of drainage stain
the measure of my feet. All
washed up, in a lather, on a soap
box, the towel thrown in.

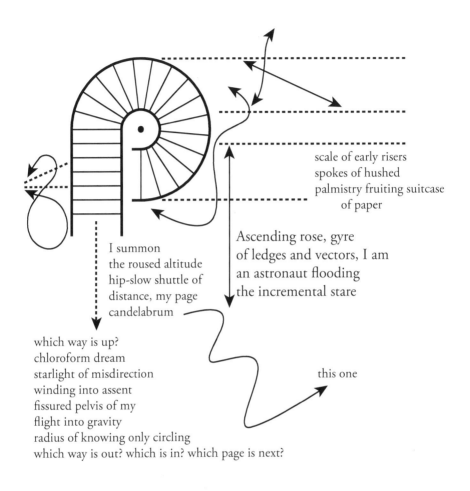

scale of early risers
spokes of hushed
palmistry fruiting suitcase
of paper

I summon
the roused altitude
hip-slow shuttle of
distance, my page
candelabrum

Ascending rose, gyre
of ledges and vectors, I am
an astronaut flooding
the incremental stare

which way is up?
chloroform dream
starlight of misdirection
winding into assent
fissured pelvis of my
flight into gravity
radius of knowing only circling
which way is out? which is in? which page is next?

this one

TULIP

Overeducated bloom
in throes of *jouissance*

The bulb swells to illuminate
a withering in the wage

All it does is grow

Infiltrations nip between
floral muscle & tumorous
assets venting from the root

Fulminating capital
contests her merosity
as not enough

Tepals a feverish grove
petaloid yet not petal
There is a difference

Brain-amulet wincing atop
a pinkish crown, her jugular
bleeding tiny leaves

All growth will be diagnosed
as too green, a skills-depleted
vitality: excelling without Excel

A new jobs program
is seeking monocot applicants

Their perfumed ache
The scholarly attitude
of their shaking perianths

What talkative talkers…
They glow on stems on a soft
green bank that is empty

It's no good

Dr. Tulip of the precariate
has entered the new
unnecessariate

FAIL SOFT

Thus, the wonderment of gently failing, like that of collapsing safely, lies in its prescience. Horoscope gland. Freckled sense replete with velar signs: letterforms, typos, all that cannot be unsaid. This drips with a natural clairvoyance, the better to decipher fluids. So, the agonies soften and the catastrophes abate and every which way, vessel-clotting, there it pillows: catchment for a glowing shatter. *Fail better.* This hill of fix and gauze awakens rouge in poultice. We are clasping swab. It takes an optimistic species of cynicism to forestall the worst.

SOFT HER (SABOTEUR)

Minimal or aside, in the form that gallantry subscripts, as sloe syrup's quiet jar, shelf-thriving in the cool. Each given sip this cobra-dope, its supple sleep guardedly unconscious. Each now-stained thought hibernal. The systems are trekking within. As in love, the fightless core. Sadly, though ferociously. Evening coincides with a grey gleam to which her solute offers. Folds sleek and essential, fern-flexing to wand among the self's own grey. This is solution's pacifism: corps of the deeper drowse, of losses inopportune, dim. Truce grieving, the shades infest.

SEMAPHORE

Our gestureless language would not confess its inaptness. Nor could the body say *quickly there are raptures against this* but with a body. Cleaving to itself in the sweet bath having said so in flexion. Washcloth releasing its tendril through soap. Our clawfoot is throbbing with water, the four-footed craft hiking the room while shadows thunder. In pain, the germ of humid thinking, chlorophyll focus. Adrift in buoyancy's lotus: a flesh-opening slowness. Heart, look to your beating. It disavows the composed sentence, remembers & pulses when languages fail.

RESERVE

Saying is latent power, the untapped cell of a battery thriving quiet. Consider my theory of holding & holding out. Skinned body of tongs, locked energy cell. Syntax incendiary but verb-less. Buried in sun, the plum-scented thralldom of nouns in a mantis grip. Jeweled deimatic wings with a blood point that flies like salmon's mouth, my blurred spit in a cup. Everything is coiled in potential, aching voltaic, pining among doers in a shroud of being. The ground like an athlete burning stamina. Fire sown a mile deep. Duration's hypnagogic seed enflamed.

FAIL SAFE

nec comedetur

Agoraphobe
  in the
agora with star
  milks
and transfusable
  code

Small cash
  basketry, counterfeit
silk worm

'On the up
  and up'
and blistering
  down

expurgated

Guile hawking
  guileless
will fail for you

How it's
  done as if
helpless

Peddling
  persiflage
in a jury-hung
  flow

Filtering threat
   less, forgetful
on cue

I launder
   the decoy
to smite myself

launch
   into
an innervated
   field
of camouflage

where each
   guise
lights a pain
   point

I'm a
   sullen
venture
   in various hues
of scorpion

voting
   on market
deluge
   inside rapturous
jackets

the skills-poll
the terror-ballot

I'm told aspiration endangers
  what my gaffe mitigates
when power outage frees
  lovely foams & ballast

I qualify
  for a jobless
unelectable
  monsoon

Fervour
  touches
internally
  its strenuous
backfires

Or dreams
  beyond speech
therapy

to viverrid
  ambition

PHANTOM LIMB

Mourning is the bond
of epiphysis: bone theory
moving in the notch.

The intimate other
in frictional gossip.

Sanction portions
torsions lather & low

epithet
by epithet:

the dead &
the nearly dead
in cartilaginous pseudo-bond.

What's left is the single
bite—
flowering bone.

How it flirts with
the *os* imperceptible.

How it moves in consonance.

Pin-gargle, antiphonal suite
between swallowed sharps
& foliated cup.

Songs genuflect
in fractal form.

The score's filament frees
itself in recursion. That is

its identity:
again& a gain increasing.

Sonation licks
from the operculum:

an aperture
a suctioning moat.

Filament slipcase, dermal
juju & the edible mallows
that fluke through.

Speak *syringe*
in flavoured language.

Make substitutions.

Girdle & hope.

SEMANTOGRAPHY

FIRST BLISS

collect the fundamentals of communication (w5h)

? ʌ ~~the cellular cypher is reluctance, a narrator~~
~~invented by a pattern of questioning~~

? ~~he, softly, persistently, somberly, officially~~
~~so as to solicit compliance, memorably so~~

? ~~in the infinite recumbence, the marrow, a~~
~~a vestigial philtrum, an odour, crab-held~~

? ◷ ~~at the appointed time, in a snatched~~
~~moment, carefully recorded, then & always~~

? ▷ ~~because despite notwithstanding and yet~~
~~why yes in the furtherance of peace~~

? ^ ~~through its fluids, markings & silence, its~~
~~gratuitous grasp of what's happening, its~~
~~deft medicinal vision, shattered, evidential~~
~~as though swabbed with dissection~~

what a relief is picture-idiom
discovered in looking for my speechlessness

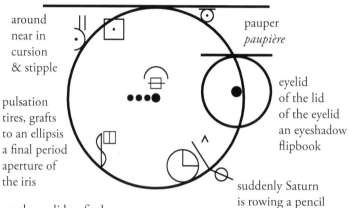

around
near in
cursion
& stipple

pauper
paupière

pulsation
tires, grafts
to an ellipsis
a final period
aperture of
the iris

eyelid
of the lid
of the eyelid
an eyeshadow
flipbook

suddenly Saturn
is rowing a pencil

open the eyelid to find
asylum in a book's
internal medicine

code for writing time
for the action of composing
a clock's pie chart
our shy phatic code

concentric relation
mutates beyond center
the pilot lights are
landing in the eyes

THIRD BLISS

the imaginary wakens
within nerved proliferations

[1] siphoned [2] eye
[3] caldera of [4] fur
[5] translations
[6] pour [7] electric
[8] shout [9] hmmm...

MITIGATION

A fail safe is a design
feature that anticipates
suffering, botch, injury
& sinister beguilement
& so maintains safety
in the midst of risk or ruin.

DEAD MAN'S SWITCH

the doctor says
let go just let
go and it will
stop

accelerating to the application of brakes
opening to the vest of a new bomb
snicking clear and few the hourly rescue

ELEGANT DEGRADATION

this cedar machine
that cleaves through scent
the way of burnished breaking
infested, clogging, toppling
in slow motion so the tree
for a time still works

FREE RETURN TRAJECTORY

they engage deep space
mapping, the starlight quilled
with attention, our gravity
guaranteed slingshot home
will not miscalculate
the pain of failure or the burn
angle for readmission

WATCHDOG TIMER

after failure
the dog sits the dog
stays, waits and waits
for the signal, ears cocked
and at the word it leaps up
to run again to fetch

now that its bone
has been reset

TRAPPED KEY INTERLOCKING

A developmental progression (for safe sequence control)
to ensure that the subject stands at the dilemma's crux
only after having cleared all other psychic hurdles

This key (this next key [this subsequent key {this following key
(this ensuing key [this penultimate key {and also this final key
opens} opens] opens) opens} opens] opens) opens

CROWBAR CIRCUIT

to prevent energy dilation
(overvoltage) a trisil triggered
short circuit across the output
will quiet the transfer
of power

REDUNDANT SYSTEMS (MY PALLIATION)

extra mechanisms	*(erasure)*
superfluous machines	*(palindromes)*
surplus gear	*(neologism)*
gratuitous equipment	*(centos)*
teeming substance	*(abecedaria)*
swarming stuff	*(puns)*
seething matter	*(chasm)*
boiling units	*(starchart)*
burning hordes of parts	*(recipes)*
sweltering crowds of portion	*(fossilized violins)*

FUSIBLE LINK

Spasmodic burnout There one
moment and gone the next

The alloy implements its difference
at a lower temperature Contests its
structural integrity Torn ligament
kneeling to safety Bloodhound for hot
risk-minimizing design A tiny
bone shatters & so
       a skeleton survives

TRANSITIVE

The pink-shelled Antarctic krill
are conducting like delicate fuses.

Slow skulls of drug addicts turn
heliotropic to the burning stove ring.

Without nearing, an owl touches with
leatherette fear the dying birdwatcher.

The woman's convolvulaceous clutch
is pursed around a pittance.

In cities, astonished emojis fail
their cellular missions, but like pearlescent

custard internally sensed, her milky
corpuscles are drifting in lymph.

MOUTHFEEL

SENSORY INDEX

A lexicon to distinguish between the various rheological properties of matter inside the mouth: beyond the philtrum, in the vestibule, encamped on the soft palate. These terms express how the mouth senses or intuits the fluttering conquistador, *the alimentary bolus.*

Agon point	Moisture absorption
Bite uniformity	Moisture release
Cohesion	Mouthcoating
Density	Roughness
Excitation	Slipperiness
Fracturability	Smoothness
Graininess	Uniformity of chew
Gumminess	Viscosity
Hardness	Wetness
Heaviness	Anosmia

As the list illustrates, the mouth's sensory apparatus is concerned with struggle. It perceives rupture, succulence, thralldom, pleasure & paradox. It is inhabited by power, by settlement, resistance, desire. At any given moment, there might be, inside the mouth, soft tams of pomegranate or sticky griefs exuding from dates. Mouthfeel registers & calibrates this immeasurable inner theatre *so that it might occupy language.*

BITE UNIFORMITY

Day catapults at dawn, tripling with heat
then turtling into the dirt

The dead kilted, hatching
teeth in the peat

Strata kittening, buckle-tight, cuticle rucked-up
to cowl over the vixen that drags the unflowering
egg to rock

Furthering, grotty, bear-down

This is burial's tactility: a tooth's coagulating
pulp chamber, secret, pain-schistic

Nerves are drastic, skittering
through gaslight

Their tentacle-beauty, suction-tusk,
bashing the tissues

Starlight at the loch
the kirk's crystalline
bodycount scalded in salt

The saint the swallowgod
that saves the blue
terabyte of blood data

MOISTURE RELEASE

decipher the sleeping hot
spliff a dexterous smoke
half aspirated ghost

whispering, the interval
peels the trade muscle

resplendent taxations
sclerotic blue glass
ulcer in a financed light

some taste splays
in a blissed-out emulsion
the succulence is bristling

even the spiked colostrum
slobber velociraptor
they are displaced in the host
century of our body

even the plaster cast
of a spleen seeks now inward

to the forest placenta
milks' perturbation
the ovum-suckling wilds

Hesperides that smell of Pink
Lady apples assimilated
over the core flesh

MOISTURE ABSORPTION

our thorn thickening usher flouts within sheaves of of
holds the wived histamine a firstling how & with whom
our hewn shall-do washing either flashing human fish
hustling the hush-money the frowsy interior wolverine
take this heckled schist of vowels hordes of shame hunt
now harshly within ourself hedged sound of showering
our leash will hasten ruination the floorfur a cathected
touch-field we fuel & furl into it ur-thinkingly as ferned
collations thick & flume we are whistling rhythmic this
aeration thwarts you wet a theory flush with suncushion
fieldbury threads or threats of hot if-throbbing sugar

EXCITATION

Pewter fusilier repletion
Lodge upon heatwave
Pluck a rosaceous scenting-gun
Emboss rustbelts of svelte hinterland
A flecked ebon hoosier
Vision's factorial gorging
Reifies resistible flak jacket
Glassine in castaway corsetry
Genderless white shark tasting
Gill as the ounce of oil from an inkling
Burst *ivresse*
A fibrillating snow-foam
Tender the shrapnel of clemency
Accelerant, do fear me
I have bladders of hastening gradient
Crow-sloughs & tipping-points
Soft lashing ganders incise me
A blushing gustatory remnant
Is ashfully increasing

AGON POINT

Glottal surge, para-filial
flange meta-gargling *Uncle!*

Know the truism of the prawn-
laved homunculus

held thrift among swoon
against *blaupunkt* plenitude

Thinking equivocates
an augered *feng shui*

or bickering guy-wire
blazing taught

Unfathomable crags
of clusterfuck

adhere to a ricked impulse

to busk among thieves
to walk a gangplank sensorium

of coruscating mouthgag
& lithium hoodwink

punctum
scotoma

Integument immersed
in mood's biotic gloss

My histrionic volta
fishtails through tea leaves

Regale me with augury, amorphous gorge

Pulk me through the halved axiom

§

Beside me the *Nissin Dental
Model* is a burst hawk:

Split jaw of raptor talons open on
a fulcrum for the hygiene student

Silver tools into lacquer
hunting imagined rot

Crisping, flushing, whispering
doubling with mouth mirrors

Bearing pastes & amalgams
stick-handling spatulas

Delving, cornering with honed
curettes & root explorers

in sensual
co-lingual terrorism

Model talker, subliminal
huntress, war hawk, revolt

Sky-sumptuous, say the word

WETNESS

slurred rhotic purr
star liquors
dissolving hospice
reeling apostolic
the slender milks
gilled and breathing
in the jostling
missile silos, the snicks
and cluster
of velar suffusion
aurora borealis
drips like hunger
sloe plums glister
askance in a wasp lair

§

blow-worlds & pluralisms
earlier fleets of proto-porcelain
roaring, the risk of Rieslings
of rarely slaked
listening
aching fossorial psyche
caterwauling flurry to storm
stow form in valvular
blood-flume, hell's bells
we are whistling disparate
to holster conciliation
in pleather fist-folds

UNIFORMITY OF CHEW

diagnosed ovary
permeable rose histamine

denigrated
we overproduce

the mouth-eye's
translucence reveals
a gibbering tusk

emergent in the fire-
climax in burn-
pocked furze

startled, we shuck
insolence with a liquefied
half-laugh

gull into swale
as the million hillsides

antler with *owls*
a feverish black

angle decelerating
gut filibuster

the sugaring omen
is a keening spiracle

VISCOSITY

my cudgel's obstreperous

a racketeer engrossed
in obfuscation

the sixth isthmus
the scolded genre

my protuberance struggles
against itself

regularly
gracelessly

reiterate, for example
these flabbergasting maxims
faster and faster:

"pad kid poured curd pulled cod"

"Eiffel's authored ether fossil us sufficeth"

"pearls blurred in a foul vowel prayer"

"the glibbest of crisp gibberish"
"the glibbest of crisp gibberish"
"the glibbest of crisp gibberish"

faster!

"a feral velar flail,"
apparatchik!

SLIPPERINESS

crisp existing fallow
the aspirated swarm
its liquidity concussed
in seismic storm
torrential whet rasping
& long e r o s i o n a l sculling
so grasp the capsid of formula
in wild plasmatic fascicle
as if language could surface
its own organ or slake
its ridge with tremulants

ANOSMIA

I

Since I do not smell I do
not taste and the comet in my mouth
is hot or cold, the spoon bled
snow or piping *matcha* is only
in this moment its temperature, and
its tail
thrusters dissolve and disclose
a slender revolt: the sixty green eyes
and soft thirty tongues
glaring up from space

II

wasabi lip-sear Scoville stab-nose Komodo Dragon
capsaicinoid in ghost chile ransom *habanero* pain a
sweating *harissa* shiv red *som tam* heat-sensing
trigeminal ka-pow slit *Naga* viper and scorpion
organoleptic wince *sriracha malagueta* fume-shrill
chiltepin-burn infinity reaper howl the eel foaming ow
cherry-flecked blood rush of *bhut jolokia* endorphin
sob dropkick *fatalii* resiniferatoxin bee sting nasal bite
apricot iguana bomb face-wrath of the pin-hiking
sun nerved with fruit and claw the cultic pang of it

III

the face stands amazed
carbonation's burr is like
light-thistle or joy, the pedigree
of surprise sensed in the well
behind the nose, in the throat's
wall spackled with pep
there is some talk
of inoculation and cattails
while the after-prickle subsides

IV

Salt cyanotype Pensive
distributions of bitterness
This worthless sugar touch Immersed I am
diabetic in my craving sodium-mad
and hypertensive drinking vinegar
to think about that tang
running like a cougar glint-faced
and ulterior thicking venom to suck
on blistering phosphor

V

grief eating glow-syrups the meta-delectation now at a
fever pitch swigging the imago your drenched flagon of
tarrying wolves flowing in sexpacks round and round it
noumenal whiff without *umami* scow crest resounding
the dictum of a pelt-opening fur greased punk face in
some sorrow limb by limb the savourless *dim sum* its
velvet threat feasting in your mouth spermatozoa and
spore-cleft steeply loss as if a blossom thicket could
haunt the mouth blank sensing texture where it inhales

.

READING JOURNAL

I wake to the sound of the garbage
truck grinding through the back lane.
Beside me, a black fur cushion gives a heavy
sigh, fluttering its ears. The soft tight oval
would spring apart, paws and tail, if I made
the slightest move—then beg for food.
Guilty, I stay very still. I make
a sleepy sound. I roll over.

An hour later I read the first six pages of *Seeing
Red* by Palestinian-Chilean writer, Lina Meruane,
whose speaker, Lucina, is like a dangerously full
glass of blood, delicate as a thin-hulled bulb
about to burst: *The carnal throes of passion
were forbidden, because even an ardent
kiss could cause my veins to burst. They were
brittle, those veins that sprouted from my retina…*

§

I think of *Seeing Red* as *Seeing
Read* & remember the old
newspaper joke: *What's black & white
& read all over?* If it bleeds it leads. But reading
is like that: carnivorous, bloody-minded,
bursting, blood-thirsty. When dried,
carnelian. Reading is messy. It likes
the brink, walks the gangplank, & sails
risk to see what it can see. Its ship is not
at sea upon the crimson

but barely contains it. It is ready
at any moment to detonate
the vessel & spread
all that can be red.

§

I switch to earthy, violent Aase Berg, whose *Transfer*
Fat is so full of Swedish puns that translator Johannes
Göransson must conjure a strange election
to accommodate all the canny slippage. The word *val*
means whale, election or choice: *You Voter chose*
this licking smelting star... I imagine the whale
weighing in on the fate of rising oceans. It has only
itself, & all the other whales of voting age, to blame.

§

We like to suckle animals, egg animals, whalenut animals

§

What policies do whales prioritize? Are they
partisan? Have they read their Melville
& what would a whale review
of *Moby Dick* en-tail?

§

I unlatch the top lock, the bottom lock, the dead
bolt in the middle, & free my dog to the backyard
of my ex's house where I pet-sit our mutt. He looks
most vulnerable, most pitiful, when he squats
somewhere in the back beside the stars of frayed
rhubarb, their stems a watery blood pulsing toward

bright fuscia veins. Locked in this primordial
pose, the furrow of his being hovering in the act
of expulsion, my dog ingests the sunlight, & it
is this inclusion, in each black hair, in each follicle
of becoming, that allows me to see him.

§

Hovering over my silver, food-flecked
laptop, spattered with dark brackets
of dog fur, I click through a series of unreal
folders. Digital metaphors for containment
for filing in a 'paperless' domain. I apply
to coordinate a youth program. I apply
to teach in Michigan. I indulge
a feeling of futility. I return
to my volunteer work.

§

At five o'clock. I fantasize about writing an article for *Cabinet*
magazine. I brainstorm titles: The Anthropophagy of the Tongue-
lovers (We Would Like to Eat Your Language); The Infinitesimal
Viability of Largesse in Straitened Times (A Curveball); How I Love
You, Effervescence. First the title, then the article: this constraint.
For example, a history of carbonation in the beverage industry (the
many ways that fizziness has been marketed). An artist's project
about colonial language erasure that marks lexical excision with
illustrations of prepared cold tongue. Every missing word is organ
meat. Or, worst of all, fetish-worthy data charts of charitable
donation shortfalls during times of recession. At five oh eight,
I dismiss the idea.

§

I discover on Facebook the death-notice of a poet
I've never heard of. Then the lovely funny agony
in his poem about experimental cancer mice. He
has named all the mice Max after himself. All the
Maxes run from his cancer to my nameless, not-
fatal post-memory of your death six weeks ago,
stranger.

§

*My doctors split my tumors up and scattered them
into the bones of twelve mice.*

§

At six, I take my dog to the park. He strains
to reach three pods of dried shit, which sing
to him their origin. He spots a squirrel
& sprints after it, leaping up the tree trunk
while it clatters up to safety. He smells
an abandoned glove, pees on a patch
of flowers, rolls in the cool grass, scrunching
his snout into green. When he sees a torn
bird-wing, alone in stalled flight across the earth,
he wags his tail & races to the amputation.

§

Forty-five minutes later, I braise
the kale, pour the wine, mince the garlic,
char the chicken, steam the rice, eat
the meal, alone, while checking Twitter.

§

At 20:20:41, I begin reading page 63
of *Beast Feast* by Cody-Rose Clevidence
whose name rhymes providentially
with "evidence."—*the bulls are claustrophobic,*
ringing—a smothering regeneration in which
I am the petaluminescent excrementious void of a reply—
throbbing in the steam without larynx
& the flesh is a shared text about
to tighten into a fist, scatter & fly.

§

I do not remember what happens next.
For twenty-five minutes, I do something
that I have forgotten.

§

Then I tweet
about what I have read, which
nobody notices. Because I have no
followers. My dog sniffs
and licks my foot.

§

At eleven, I peel open the concentric skin
of *Broom Broom*. The coiffed, concentric
mind of *Broom Broom*. So like an onion
with its bevy of heads. And read
about bathtubs.

§

Mayans plumb the first pressurized water feature
in the new world and inscribe tubs with an astrological
cartography, atlas to the waterways of beyond.

§

In a dream that night, I open my head. Prying through waved
hair, lit glossy, mid-century, I snap my skull apart. —*Click*—. And mouse
over the female head icon. —*Double-click*—. There is a terrible
scraping noise. It grows louder, grating the inside of my skull. There is
something in the wall. A mouse. I look at the dove-grey drywall & spot
a curved line, nearly worn through, growing thinner & thinner
as the mouse chews. —*Click-click*—. The icon decocts. I fall
asleep & fake-wake when a man emerges from the wall & puts
his arms around me. We bathe in blankets. Can I stay? he asks.
The SWAT team has arrived. Weapons alert. The man
should not have chewed into the house. I should not
have opened the folder. Should not have read.

SURVEY

In order to better swerve you, please and sir the flowing quest
narratives. Circumnavigate the resplendent that best deflects
your exponential growth.

1. The library contains
     a. yes
     b. no

2. What I read in the library
     a. is the gorgeous snack of babes, swiftly digested
     b. teaches me to know the brain that lunches here
     c. saves itself over & over with beefed-up catalogue
     d. proves that I am hungry

3. I wish the library would
     a. kiss me full on the mouth with the ferocity of love
     b. pet me sensually beneath the pages
     c. put the toilet seat down!
     d. fight with me so that we can have make-up sex

4. The last book I read at the library was
     a. *The Last of the Mohair*
     b. *Alligator Sly*
     c. *The Feminine Mistake*
     d. *All's Quiet on the Well-Built Front*

5. Overdue fins
     a. smell fishy even when fresh
     b. clench the plate like the ragged suckers of octopi
     c. fill me with greed for better time manliness
     d. swim to me with breathtaking translucence, as if invisible

6. I find the nose-level in the library
    a. suspicious
    b. intrusive & way too curious
    c. lower than I expected, given how tall the shelves are
    d. swashbuckling, in the seductive manner of Cyrano

7. I come to the library for
    a. back-breaking birth
    b. the impetus of culture, evolving its taste
    c. the handsome shelver, whose hands could shelve me
    d. forensic evidence

We look forlorn to severing you aghast here at
The Pubic Livery

CONTRACEPTIVES

ABSTINENCE

When you willfully
resist the allurements
of music, when you
smother your cries in the pillow

CERVICAL CAP (DIAPHRAGM)

When you swallow a spring
(-loaded cap) so that no
speech or breath exudes
from your larynx

THE WITHDRAWL METHOD

When you slow and elongate
your vowels in the nick of time
to prevent impregnation

THE RHYTHM METHOD

When you regulate the cadence
of your cries to ensure
that none may germinate

CLADE OF ANALGESICS

MORPHINE

Enter the god 'rayed
in poured endorphin
Relief is a minor lunacy
Come push ccs

of pain-
less
kite

They
describe
the
sky

An ethe-
real
excur-
sion

A love-
ly ful-
gent
scour

MORPHEUS

Sleeping affirms
a night-gesture: dreaming

There's a fresh
cut in the sediment
from which colostrum
clouds:

Nightmare and capeline
thickness and vigor

MORPHING

Protean task
of mulling

Direction tilting
to the lake effect

A scene-stalked
siege of eyelids

The brilliant
blinking cinema

My comatose
arpeggio

TWENTY-FIRST-CENTURY MACHINE

star counter-shade violet gland
hock crest and flews
carpals communal pad *rete*
mirabilis in the carotid sinus
ligament winching the back
axis to a spinous process blunt
vertebrae fur-trimmed pendant
ear and mesocephalic lunge
dichromat and visual streak
fumble and dewclaws sweet
patch of gums scarred snout
anus tail bite sprinting bark

ODOUR THESAURUS

SUGGESTED TERM (ADJ.)	*COMPOUND DESCRIPTION FROM CLINICAL STUDY*
APESTIC	A smell that repels young women and attracts the African Wild Dog. Perspiration, primordial festering and fear, pustules and small cuts in the dorsal muscle, lipids consumed by sharp-scented bacteria.
BRATHY	Barbiturates and hash, maybe, or percolating cola, a clangor of carbonation, or something held for three long weeks in the pocket of a guru yogically flying from the precincts of Haight-Ashbury in the late 60s
CORROIDAL	Caustic cash insolvency. It lingers. A corona of bitter trash and adolescent bilge, ammonial perfumes steeped in rising debris, our plan to clean and re-finance next month.

DISFARAL Dispersed wood mist, aging
understory, or maybe a resinous
cedar-spell freshened with fetish
like the day we walked in circles
pursuing coastal rains

ERETORY Everything with salt
everything with a grain
everything pickled and
pressurized

FERVIN Flayed oysters, crab-
heart machined in the teeth
the horn of a narwhal
the ocean pleat

GULLING Gypsum, purblind grief
of chromium, a cool metallic
winter. The taste of lace
is spreading its holes down
the larynx, and hourly (petiolatedly)
its ornamental language.

HESPERY	Heat wave sweat-spike, oil spatter, virginity on cotton, mussels that swallow a sting of *nam pla* slick with lime

IRASCID	Inside ancient pharmacal tuns a tuberous hale meditation: Starches. Tonics. Grassnotes. Herbaceous cordials or soft-deke sage. Mourned sip we might guess. Hold a plum-pit, grief counselor, marination in the mouth, a resonant scotchy phenol. In green glass the weedy *Jägermeisters* are blowing brackish. Hunted pearlescence, *digestif.*

JABBLY   Jelly fruit brio, red radio
                  tang. I remember the crust
                  of certain coagulating syrups
                  made of innards simmering down
                  fraise, balsamico, gigantesque
                  I am slathering frisky *compote*
                  when I see me

KARSIC   Kool-Aid in the stain, Kool-Aid
                  in the glass pitcher that weeps
                  with condensate, Kool-Aid
                  in the sugar spray from a slit
                  foil packet of eyes

LUPID   Lice in a corrupt comb, floss decay, dope
                  in a blister pack, anodyne syringe
                  tip, barely chloroform, our failing discipline

MARDISH	Marinate in soil. Take steak born inside blood and cellophane, born under wraps, and roll it in the garden. Monthly. An old blush of murk and menstruum, tampon in pebble dust, lost there and kicked around some, that small sad worm-death, detonated rub of night beetles.
NUMINANT	Nicotine edged with peat moss, Novocain and garlic, wood-smoked sutures over a swale of brine, the pong shadowing *kimchi* down alleyways of burning newsprint
OLFEOUS	Otter-pelt rank, burning pearl and lake water, hail in your hair with faint gooseberry styling gels, pulsed aquarium of drowning muskrats

PRISTILINE   Pyrex disproof, glassy neutrality
                  of this here whereness
                  hotel lobby, a scentless rejection
                  the brisk terror inside the quarantine
                  room, a lonely pheromonal vacuum

QUEROUS   Quizzical carpet, unknowable
                  the home into which
                  I have not yet moved. A brown
                  plastic doll in a suede dress.
                  Without fire. Without passport
                  or breath. But feathered.
                  Fringed. In a wall-to-wall unit
                  of accordion doors & worn
                  linoleum. With blue-scented eyes

RISPID   Rapid shinbone, tail-
                  slate, mineral and chalk, dust
                  breathing from the hairy vents
                  granules and eyelashes, scale and
                  ash, deep salty pits, everything
                  rejected and swept away
                  hot furtive laundry

SILVEOUS   Stink of bourbon, incursion, sweet-breath.
Like Soho in the 50s. Notes of feral page count, velvet
curtain, street bleed. We have entered the vellum and
the booze. Now we are writing about dissipation.

TANTROUS   The rancid calyx
of your mouth is hiccupping whiskey
the detonation of oil
and anchovy, something
or other incessantly
breathing its red herring

URLIQUIOUS   Undulant peals of tropic, tanning bronzer
skin-warm and silicate, a coral
aragonite with hints of coconut
sexuality, bikini-fresh clangour
infectious cultures of curvature

VERNISSED Viridian lid, concealer.
Shelves of henna, and Max
Factor. Lacquers of Dior
Nail Glow, pink seed-
scented *maquillage* and a spritz
of ambergris. Consider
the *summa* of parabens
and parfum: diethyl
phthalate, antimicrobial esters.

WELTISH Wiggly pink Jell-O
marks the too-high
transom of a school (*Le Colibri*)
doors locked around the lesson
of her excellence. In the dream
whales levitate through
the smell of bologna

XYPHIC Xeric, sclerotic, ping. As if made of dried
juniper and coal-deep currants. As if
a weather-strip of pemmican were laced
with snow cherry and toasted in sunlight.

YEWING Yolk
exploding
with a yellow scent
Softcore salt
Melted butter stick

ZOUR Zest, sweet gall, roasted
flanks of derma and their burning
skill saw, peruke in ash
scampi and flayed
choral smoke

OR(E

The ancient planetary

body
gushing in its closet

has been struck
many times

and holds now
between

its many sheaves
an ill-tempered
chronicle

of being
& the condition

of being
in the shape
of its mineral

record among
various cloths &
materialities

This grandeur

is an intimacy

stoked by fire
& geology

held among
shoes and their
soles & laces

the ore
immoveable

or squirming
in the dark

I

Archaean gold, arkose, clasts of minutely
Suspended air, the oxygen dispersed
But held with mineral deliberation.

At the shatter-cone, bone-cyst, impact glass
And ejecta. The tooth of a meteor cawed
Through its thunder.

From within, plutonic pillow breccias, flesh
Of my comb. The eye slits open to terrify
The shores of its darkness.

II

Light purrs beneath the door
a femoral fluid licking the brim.
Origami-heart. That's how night folds
like laundry around absence, like
scented cuffs in a room
locked upon systolic surgeless. A pulse
sculls along the wrists of an empty shirt.
Something moves. A cotton moth,
nearly alive, quivering down a face.

III

Ash-plain of tuff and glass, pyroclastic
substation, its ribcage a claw
gripping the heart like a bead of tephra.
What burned is now solid. A pick-axe
would perish in its cortex, fin thick
and raw as it fights to parse the core.

IV

Here are knick-knacks:
a stem of buttons, wire shins
of a shoe rack. But it's the metal
clasp that's everything, starlight
clicking with gleam. Some
lightless body, closeted, some
salt, breathing. Listening
for the okay.

V

Slow cobalt blood-back,
pithy conciliation. A keel
in the breast falls inward to rest
at the saddle point of hyperbole.
Stems drain beneath a sleek pyrethrum
athrob with the ardor of scent. Strum
the sob of cryptic plumage, to render
as alloy, burnt opulence.

VI

Count shoes, eyelets, pebbles.
Smell leather, vinyl, sure-
footedness. Crouch
over toes.

VII

Tungsten, wolf
cream: slow-mo
on a lick of metal.

Wolves curdle and
collect—*lupi spuma*
—with the body's

words for *body*.
They throat down
the elegance with which

they affirm
urged by heat
and compression

to sinter a spine.
They embed and
conduct. They gear

up. Unmeltable,
with licked claws
and power, wolfram

steals into veins
and abyssal fractures
howling into rock

in compound
to seed the earth's
lupine bloom.

VIII

Shell. Egoist, abalone
engrossed by its own silver ear
sitting cross-legged with music
Stain invisible inside another stain
Sound lacquered upon water

IX

Silversword asleep in the flow zone.
Frosted anemone on a bed of cinder.

Its rays prickle the air, toss their floss
to the know-how of the howling wind

kick and hustle like rarity on the blent
wreckage of high-altitude fires. Its silver

bursts, draws a line of shrapnel from core
to tip. That sprig of ballistics will keen

and slit each thought, tracing its path
to the limits of what can be known.

On the slopes of Haleakala, cold as ozone,
a mind taps the ashen mother lode.

Quiet as cosmos and lonely and sharp
as the genius of stars.

X

& the room slams around itself
With darkness quarries the mind

As Egyptian embalmers
wishing to parse immortality
handle an obsidian
scalpel

XI

Men arrive, transgenic,
unslakeable. They are
fleet and immersive. They gently distend
diaphragm and throat, syrinx flexed
like a chord of magma swallowing
its own heat. Light travels in shadow:
forked tongue, internal bird, a slit blaze
glazed in char. Cartilage and bone
are bright albinism of a crow.

XII

Swallow
Sleepdeep
Skinned
knee Wing
beat

XIII

Assembly, florilegia. The moon's
glossy oculus bathing compacted
strata. The layers and layers
in recursion. Geology's thug
of mineral echo, pierced
by planetary drama, pelted,
struggling, impressed.
Where bones engrave, soft
ligatures vacate and their feathers
and sinkholes and blades
made of heart muscle. But some
flexed momentous itch stays
hitched in the echelons.
Its progeny in fixed
furious gravure.

XIV

Soft susceptible
omnibus, take your page
to the mouth of the opening
door. Make a paper
face and burn
the lease when it swings
to close again.

A PINK HOUSE

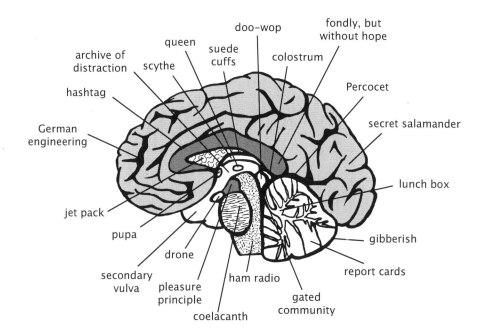

The queen, like her secondary vulva, was a product of enhanced German engineering. Nestled in suede cuffs, she could think. The patter of report cards was gibberish. It was doo-wop she heard, snug as a scythe, making musical cuts in her secret salamander. With her jet pack she could fly through the Percocet, into a gated community filled with colostrum, and listen. An archive of distraction, ornamented with hashtags, awaited her—and, just east of drone, a ham radio tuned like a lunch box. Here, with the pleasure of principle, she unwound like a coelacanth into the pink house, fishing fondly, but without hope, for some pearlescent pupa, burning in the buzz.

BESIDE HER SELF

NEXT OF KIN

dextral & sinistral slight venom along the
mirror line between you & your sister
slicked off with oil & a bronze strigil
each softness will sting without cut or
vale the faces amplified & reversed the
flesh caustic & lung each held in a fox-
beautifying light a fond puck of madness
courses between in the shape of a throb
alchemical depth charge softly nostrum

you are some
soft where in me
the smoke of you
chafing my lungs
your smoulder
a spore that will not
grow so the curse
between us is that
you will appear
only if I die

HER PROXY

cedar pang in the memoir this convoy of
wood-scented alibis how each symphysis
binds absence to absence like the bone
fixed between orbits these vocal folds
opulent and still as if to nominate an
other in the place of one's own eyes or
larynx lounging on code reinforced by
rust blood ignites corrosion's ovary spits
hunger & a red rumour of eggs

*I've tried to summon
you inside a stopped
elevator using panic
and ploy imagining
you speaking
finally for me*

HOW TO HIDE IN PLAIN SIGHT

spokes & leathers & kittens of might a
missing missive attachment that should
cling as the loved postage enveloping
twin within twin wasn't that you among
the guile your burst lining fitfully awry?
our similar tongues mistaken between to
bleed our loveliest pleather o sister we'll
skin the enclosure with a honey blade
talk the talk & lookalike our stun

*I look but am not
like you I circulate
but do not know anything I
haemorrhage but have never
been opened*

CURING

atavistic saltpan a brain-white light into
pain's optic rappel etiology & star-gut
suss the vatic plenitude the sister now
burning in the sunspot without meaning
her brine stockpiling language to swim
in our hut-sigh heat wave stung geyser
sodium stasis & puppet foam the body
altared now preying on hymn its edifice
smoked salted & irritatingly apostolic

*I case the joint as a critic
would read the symptoms
of a coded book about
eccentric codes*

HOMUNCULUS

o you animalcule poached in vestibular
slow cookery sharpshooting the rumour
of your existence do you feel from the
inside the pressure to maximize to rise &
foment idling into the rapturous salvo of
miniatures mouthing grandiloquence or
without size will you move from minor
to major through pestilential style cutting
your teeth on its virulence?

the legacy is
a conspiracy of tenterhooks
there hangs in me
an astonishing tenderness
for the voice thrown
or given over
like poetic infection all my
compaction intact beneath
your sumptuousness

HER INKY FINGERS

phloem sweet & vascular so the lisping
glans of the writing act pulsing to the
distal fringe at the fingerprints there's an
anchorite laced throughout the apsis
both near and far from direction her
influence sprays onto a screen like the
noirish laugh of a suddenly superpose-
able sister whose projected voice now
sips from a cloister of ripening buries

the body glandular
botanical an anchor
by which you are deeply
impressed so radical
I sense the burial
bursting though

CODPIECE

pouch on the seamount of wet trousers
the Minoan culture clothed in minnows
thousands of years before the dorsal &
caudal fins of grieved codlings swept
through the collective unconsciousness
of our mouths gummed up in saltwater
taffy a snout's emphasis below the cote
slim propulsion of the tongue which will
change colour when it's in too deep

you're an infant a
treachery a spoke
in the wheel of language
you fish among waste-
bands with the infinity
of your tongue

OWL KNOWLEDGE

portent in spelling a talon-eyed hunter
scans the lexicon art of the artery the
orb we absorb a seer's gift from distant
astronomies the mossy hag in sphagnum
ageless & phenolic the long-ago dragons
lighting tinder of their tongues over a
stash of hoarded pronouns beneath the
surface the sun alive in the eon's sunken
galleon now the willed omen of women

*nothing can struggle
in you like the in
visible the unfathomed
home for war*

OMEGA

a fabric sacrificially soaked what is left
surrendering its face the axons fire into
the nervous system of a chemical lace
schizophrenic solution to burn it away to
lay claim to a tinged hermaphroditic core
an emulsive merger of her & her (& hymn)
as a new electrical identity begin research
begin basic training learn tactical man-
oeuvres for how to balance the inner salt

*everything about you
is about me and together
how utterly our mutual
ellipsis will sing*

HER BLUSHING TONGUE

colossal lace of lilies necking along the
frenulum let us touch with pliancy what
we know of ourselves now stalking the
filament of our bulbs with cordiality
among lightless glass blossoming in the
mouth at the deep end of our language
where the overture violates the rule &
the body reads a vestigial fuse radiance
swarms & pollinates the stellar nursery

like my dream of you
in the blue
version of my gold
dress invisible in the room
but suddenly there
in the mirror where all
of my power foams
can I count on you
to become a lightning flash
calibrating lumens in the pan
spermia

STEAM STORIES

head-caw   wraith

of later   pierced now

lamplust

and its smog

for seeing   the dark

sequester in lean

muscle   slight hairs

of thinking

skin   towards cold and

look terror   clean

the licking soul

three jump rope   at a time

coefficiencies   of snow

golfed into

the pond

gestating   fresh among star

in a salt

panicked ocean

coin at the notch
a bloodfarm thickening
iteration

take soft we will
toughen our pasts

thriving on the body
of that money

this, and
another altogether
luminous fossa
worth licking

subtleties capitulate
in musk our
halogens gasp

soak bright	*water*	~~grief-shrug~~
hematoma	*fall*	~~a form~~
the cellfrost	*potent*	~~fitting~~
of blood	*iality*	~~smooth~~
that summation	*is not a let*	~~after~~
electrically hoping	*down*	~~math~~

intricacies turned on liquid energy an added loss

paper sutures
that intangible

our homeland of steam
leaflets red in a void

first foray of this spaceship
moving diffuse through star-ponds
at a rate gathering anchor

night-stall, thrusterless
riverine float

our loon-heat, galactic
the kettle-boiling breath

in our capsule

a pick silvers
opening raw in water

variable shoulder
of pine shade sleeks
beyond solvency

canyons ankle
forward in bold thrift
to swell with lake value

superfluity of eyelids
deep nerve locus

a lichen storm
edits translucence
with looking

to see the cashed-out
sorrows curvatures
snuffling heat from heat

the live wire pulsing home

gunlovely dawns
shot scarlet

entrails perforated
to phrase portions

in every mouth
cherries dilate

sonar residues
haunt us between

on a screen softer
than infancy

stars narrow
the forcefield

magnetized large
celestial bodies

we draw
imperceptibly
nearer

milk shell
fluxed fever

once warm thousands
in a hill of sand

a sort of fracturing
everywhere

the evening sociopathic

what follows in lion
furred seeming

is the mane of a hand
devouring on a blood
stain at night

alongside
the fingers

those teeth
cream locus

of pales
that qualm here

if these opals
soak through me

will I remember
to feel them?

A DIFFUSION IN ROWS & COLUMNS

canvas-backed
    heart   totebag of   etiolated
                                                  blooms

ship clawed
    spasmodic   a child   suffused
                                                  with hawks

threnody's
    milky   thrum   between coma
                                                  and semiosis

erosions
    oblate   and supple   a conjugal
                                                  sulk

so ardently
    asleep   so wetly   piscine it
                                                  suspects itself

alveolar
    killing   jar   wing-hooks
                                                  in the din

soothsayers
    disclose   the true   nature
                                                  of writing:

glow-body
    a solemn   ether   syllables at last
                                                  gasping

white cot

                      alert

                                                with pins

APPLICANT

COVERLET

the candidate is scented foam

burst crocus throat
battling inception with its
army of foals

a dress made of dendrites
is now draping the soma

where it gathers on pre-leather
skins, transmissions
contrapuntally fume

smoke at each sync-
point makes lovely
the insinuation

(glossed w/ footnotes)
of barbs and book-learning

select keywords
for the position

sought: *parsed griefwork, Girl
Friday ranked airborne
& corporate-lite*

those dark-lovely beguilements

into thoughtspace: my *ave*
respiring in slush

in a fug of knowing
the snapped feeling will teethe

PLEASE FIND ATTACHED MY RESUMÉ

EXPIATIONS   *birth–now*   the pulsed gossip
of my plasmid

brief miracle of myself
haunted by the past

ghosts tessellating
in ruin, the whole *sur-
face* Escher-graved

30–now   barely eluctable shoulders
architected curves deep
knowledge and data entry

now–later
(promise!)   coding and searing SEO
vanishing sleepforms
beautifying toil
bénévole

SKILL SAW   I recruit beams
            digitized brushfire
            plush bloodhound, unseen

            a click farming lethality
            amid sinuous smoke
            algorithms

            métier de mangeur, gourmandise
            elegant influencing of
            self by myself

            all the portions
            internally dovetailing
            at a pattern of precision
            cuts

            opening viscerally the seam
            into having guts

INTERNALIZATION   the subject ideally enslaved
to interview perception

money groked as human
glowingly speaking
and marriageable

oaths of allegiance, cashpoints
of sensual harm-fondling

(keywords and choir)

REIFICATIONS   1. choral reference
                    off-gassing skill

                 2. ointment, lotion
                    and stain, or salve,
                    salvage and salvation

                 3. a fountain overflows
                    with depletion-envy

                 4. droplets of graft
                    emulsifying wellness

                 5. the person who touches
                    me knows
                    my worth

INTERVENE

Please hesitate and call

Inside the secret
clot of resumé eddies
of unpresumed power
obliterate the system

Star-fold the chasm .
of many and much

Body of my best
being do cash me
beyond currency

How leafed I have gathered
a terrifying surplus

PASTORAL

She can only want an autonomy made available by capital.
—*Anahita Jamali Rad*

speeds congressional, lovelorn
the torch burning executive heat
as hourly the body inhumes among
the underfunded stars

such glittering invertebrate beings
luminous beyond market atrocity
and deliverable only late such a lag
their priceless, unhaveable beams

the eyes snapping in their teeth
they voyage through the homeland
where women laden with capital roam
through whole meadows of freeloading deer

ECOLOGY

sweet pear-grit, clot-
carving through the axis in the mouth
where semiosis coagulates like sipped
chain: clawback, hook-sour, a drum sucked
sound & swallowed: the iron
oval after
oval crying iron
through seams of my mouth
time swarms with curved pleats
a vanquishing pastness, each
genesis accrual as softness born into touch
velvet machine
hunt, throbbed immersive: denizen of a thick
nap brushed over cut technology
capsize a silicone breast into its own milk
perennial fold
in soft suckling
we are falling into milk
into odorless invisible ink
into warp
& weft pares

STORM-HOOK

Helmet-look. Once upon ephemeral leap. Torch along fist,
     pounding light.
It's cortical—atavistic—the laughter of pikes can be our
     wisdom.
Deft perversity a riot scheme, lovely among hair. Tossing its
     cackle.
A deep schema of dust cloud. That nebula's plosion in sclera.
     Low haptic.
What it might & thought rising. All the skim softening touch
     will not know it.
Throat-fog—hours of launching the next slow pour—have I
     known sip of it?
Beside ourselves, in the armchair, in the overcast overcoat,
     bedazzled limit diminishing.
Sloop brisk down the up-phase of liquid, sloping notion to
     border & cruise. Two fingers
Of hot-filled stay & glass, our burning. Vanish or scintilla.
     Now hurtling.

ACKNOWLEDGEMENTS

The people who lent support and a friendly ear while I was a writing this book are too numerous to name: friends, colleagues, librarians, writer-friends, publishing-friends, family members, social media buddies, and even devil's advocates. Thanks to each of them.

While much of this book came to be in coffee shops around Calgary (thanks Analog, Weeds, Oolong, and Vendôme), some work just couldn't have happened without time away. I'm grateful for illuminating discussions with poet and mentor Tim Lilburn and participants and organizers of the 2017 Spring Poetry Colloquium at Sage Hill Writing Experience, where I revised this manuscript among friends and peers in the beautiful Qu'Appelle Valley. Sincere thanks also to the Sharon Drummond Memorial Scholarship and the Calgary Arts Development Authority (Artist Opportunity Grant) that together enabled me to attend. I was likewise fortunate to have attended the 2016 Spring Poetry Colloquium: Kroetsching the Long Poem, where I worked on an earlier version of "Beside Her Self." Warm thanks are due to Phil Hall and my fellow writers, and to the Alberta Foundation for the Arts, for this generative retreat.

I revised a 2012 version of "Or(e" while resident at the Banff Centre's 2013 Poetry Writing Studio, under the thoughtful mentorship of Karen Solie, Jen Hadfield, and Daljit Nagra. I give thanks to these advisors, to my fellow writers in the residency, and to the Banff Centre for the Arts, the Myra Paperny Endowment for Emerging Alberta Writers, and (once again) the Alberta Foundation for the Arts.

Thank you to George Murray for publishing "A Diffusion in Rows & Columns" on NewPoetry.ca in March 2016.

I'm also grateful to Helen Hajnoczky, Melina Cusano, and the able team at the University of Calgary Press for their care and attention in editing and designing this book.

Among the many readers, listeners, and advisors, I'd like to specifically thank and acknowledge: Noelle Allen, Chris Bassett, derek beaulieu, Natalee Caple, Weyman Chan, Nick Devlin, Carolyn Fisher, Aaron Giovannone, Carolyn Hoffman, Ian Janson, Robert Jobst, Michael Johnson, Cynthia Klaassen, Jani Krulc, Larissa Lai, Naomi K. Lewis, Marc Lynch, Shannon Maguire, Nicole Markotić, Colin Martin, Suzette Mayr, rob mclennan and Christine McNair, Lynn McLory, Lori Montgomery, Jean-Jacques Poucel, Javad Rajabioun, Natalie Simpson, Emily Ursuliak, Bob van Wegen, Angela Waldie, Janice Williamson, Chelsea Wittig, Paul Zits, the *filling Station* team, my co-conspirators in the NSWGFTIAVI (and the KP for our circular booth), and the Sheppy family (Glenn, Charmaine, Evan, Bee Garcia, Craig, Guy, Marie, Christian, Tyler and Ethan). There were readings, radio shows, invitations to publish, late-night confabulations, writing dates, offers of technical and emotional assistance, and invitations to stay while working all over the world. Thank you!

Finally, all my love and appreciation go to my mother, Estelle Dansereau, who first introduced me to poetry and bought me copies of *Alligator Pie* and books by Nicole Brossard, and who cast a careful eye over this work, raising questions and offering thoughtful edits throughout. *Merci!*

NOTES

Epigraph

The epigraph to this book is a quote from Galician poet Chus Pato mentioned by Erín Moure in "Animality and Language," her foreword to *Hordes of Writing* by Pato, translated by Moure (Ottawa: BuschekBooks, 2011).

Fail Safe

The Latin term *nec comedetur*, which begins the poem "Fail Safe," translates as 'do not be devoured.'

Semantography

"Semantography" is named for the ideographic writing system invented by Charles Bliss and described in his 1949 book of the same name. Better known by the term 'Blissymbolics,' the writing system uses a lexicon of purely visual symbols that do not correspond to spoken words or sounds. It is a "speech-less" or "unspoken" language. With Semantography, Bliss intended to create a graphical *lingua franca* defined by its basic, functional vocabulary. While the system was never widely adopted, it has been used to provide non-speakers, and people with disabilities impairing speech or language use, with the means to read and write. Because knowledge of Blissymbolics is limited to a small group of users—notably unspeaking people and their teachers and caregivers—its impact has been restricted to specialized spheres.

This poem sequence relates to a period of about one year during my childhood when I stopped speaking to anyone except my mother. As such, it concerns (apparently chosen or willful) speechlessness, without literally referring to a personal past.

Mitigation

Each poem in "Mitigation" relates to a particular type of fail safe: a measure or device designed to prevent catastrophe. It's worth noting that in some cases, a strategy or instrument might operate as a fail-deadly. A dead man's switch, for example, may be used not to guarantee safety, but to ensure lethality, as in the case of suicide bombers, whose suicide vests detonate when the person wearing them ceases to grip the switch, ensuring that their death or injury activates the explosives.

Poems in "Mitigation" are inspired by ideas from the article "Fail-safe" and other related articles at Wikipedia.com.

Mouthfeel

The term 'mouthfeel' refers to rheological properties: the consistency, flow and feel of something—typically food—inside the mouth. The properties listed in the poem "Sensory Index" are taken from the Wikipedia article "Mouthfeel." I have also added two of my own properties. The poem explores the mouthfeel of language itself: what feels 'sticky' or 'wet' or 'chewy' to say. Readers can best experience the "Mouthfeel" poems by speaking them aloud, so as to explore their tactility.

"Viscosity" quotes what scientists have identified as the hardest tongue twister to say, repetitiously at speed: "Pad kid poured curd pulled cod" (see Carmel Lobello, "This is the twistiest tongue twister ever, says science." *The Week* [9 December 2013]).

"Anosmia" is a condition marked by the inability to smell, and as a result, to taste. Anosmia affects approximately 1–5% of the population. Many people with anosmia can still detect basic tastes like salt, sour, sweet, bitter, and umami, but only when these are intense. Subtle flavours are completely lost (see "The Kitchen Thinker: How anosmia affects the pleasure of eating." *The Telegraph* [27 June 2014]). Other things persist: temperature sensation, texture, and feeling in the trigeminal nerve, which detects both spiciness and fizziness. According to research, anosmia can negatively impact the number of sexual partners men (but not women) have during their lifetimes—possibly because of the importance of social smelling in romantic relationships (see "Odd Reason Some Guys Have Fewer Sex Partners." *Live Science* [29 November 2012]).

Reading Journal

My poem quotes from and refers to the following works:

Chilean writer Lina Meruane's visceral novel *Seeing Red*, translated by Megan McDowell (Dallas: Deep Vellum, 2016). Courtesy of Deep Vellum Publishing.

The strange-lovely collection *Transfer Fat* (Brooklyn: Ugly Duckling Presse, 2012) by Swedish poet Aase Berg, translated by Joannes Göransson.

Cabinet Magazine, a non-profit arts and culture quarterly published in Brooklyn, New York.

From *Four Reincarnations* by Max Ritvo (Minneapolis: Milkweed Editions, 2016). Copyright © 2016 by Max Ritvo. Reprinted with permission from Milkweed Editions. milkweed.org. This haunting collection by the American poet unfortunately came to my attention only after the poet had passed away on 23 August 2016.

The aesthetically rebellious poetry of *Beast Feast* (Boise, ID: Ahsahta, 2014) by Cody-Rose Clevidence.

Brecken Hancock's Trillium-winning poetry collection *Broom Broom* (Toronto: Coach House, 2014). I also discuss the book jacket design of *Broom Broom* which features concentric identical hairstyles.

Wherever I have used a quotation from the above works, I have italicized it in my poem.

Twenty-First-Century Machine

This poem is dedicated to my dog, Rocky (beautiful machine).

Odour Thesaurus

According to research, English speakers are poor at expressing smell in language. Although humans have about 400 different smell receptors for detecting and distinguishing odours, and the ability to distinguish a trillion different scents, we confront a serious deficit when it comes to precisely expressing these in English. Explorations of these issues can be found in the following sources: "Odors are expressible in language as long as you speak the right language" by Asifa Majid & Niclas Burenhult in *Cognition* 130.2 (2014); "Judgment of Odor Intensity is Influenced by Subject's Knowledge of Odor Source" in *Chemical Senses* 26.3 (2001); "What's Up With That: Why Are Smells So Difficult to Describe in Words?" in *Wired* (11.11.14); and "English Speakers are Bad at Identifying and Describing Smells" at Smithsonian.com (28 January 2014).

To some extent, this is because English has a paucity of abstract smell-words. Instead, Anglophones often use simile to communicate odour: something smells *like* some other thing that a listener might have experienced. *Like* rotting fruit. *Like* sour milk. *Like* mown grass. Fewer English words function as do 'putrid,' 'acrid,' 'malodorant,' or 'aromatic:'

as abstract descriptions of smells. Even these few can seem almost so general as to be useless.

In "Odour Thesaurus," to make up for (or to compound) these linguistic shortcomings of the English language, I have imagined new abstract smell-adjectives.

a pink house

The brain diagram in "a pink house" is based on Plate 720 from *Gray's Anatomy* by Henry Gray (London: John William Parker, 1858).

Pastoral

The epigraph for this poem is quoted from "we are poor technicians of desire" on page 84 of *for love and autonomy* by Anahita Jamali Rad (Vancouver: Talonbooks, 2016).

Nikki Sheppy's poetry has appeared in *Event*, *Matrix*, *NewPoetry*, *Jacket2*, and *The Calgary Renaissance*, and her poetry criticism in *Arc Poetry*, *Uppercase*, and *Lemon Hound*. In 2014, Kalamalka Press published her award-winning chapbook *Grrrlhood: a ludic suite*, which meddles with math and poetry. She is a teacher, editor, and arts journalist, and serves as Managing Editor of the experimental literary magazine *filling Station*.

BRAVE & BRILLIANT SERIES

Series Editor:
Aritha van Herk, Professor, English, University of Calgary
ISSN 2371-7238 (Print) ISSN 2371-7246 (Online)

Brave & Brilliant publishes fiction, poetry, and everything in between and beyond. Bold and lively, each with its own strong and unique voice, Brave & Brilliant books entertain and engage readers with fresh and energetic approaches to storytelling and verse, in print or through innovative digital publication.

No. 1 · **The Book of Sensations**
Sheri-D Wilson

No. 2 · **Throwing the Diamond Hitch**
Emily Ursuliak

No. 3 · **Fail Safe**
Nikki Sheppy